MW01484481

BorderLine Me

BEYOND THE EDGE

ROBIN ZEE

2019

REBEL SPIRIT PUBLISHING

WWW.REBELSPIRITPUBLISHING.COM

Beautiful Terri

Never underestimate your

ability to Shine

Be Kind & go shine

love

Robin xx

DEDICATION

It is with profound gratitude that I am here today and able to write what follows in this book.

I thank my partner Sam, for being here for me during every step as this book came into being and my incredible daughter Skye who has always been my driving force and of course my friends and family. I am a work in perpetual progress.

As I worked on writing this book, it was grueling to remember and write out what happened to me. To claim it as the whole story is just not the case because I've still got more learning and life in me yet. I will just have to wait and see what else unfolds in my new found wonderful reality.

Thanks for indulging me.

My story.

For now, my journey continues. Peace and Love.

xo R.

BORDERLINE ME

THE WHOLE STORY

I can't believe I survived.

I dabbled in so many deadly situations.

I tried desperately to not think about anything, to just numb the pain, stuff all those thoughts away and take each moment as it came.

I never felt worthy of anything, nor did I know how to change what was.

So, I pushed the limits because I didn't care what the consequences were.

Life had been a nightmare for as long as I can remember.

This is my story.

xox

Robin

THE DARK SIDE

I wrote this on April 9, 1998.

Missing pieces from long ago leaves emptiness.

Wondering, pondering in the darkness, a vast space of incomplete.

Someone knows, but can't, or won't, go back there, even though it could provide me with some relief.

Angered & hurt by their unwillingness to even try, to set theirs aside on my behalf.

No effort in sight, as I scream for relief; the slightest recall would help me.

My cries fall on deaf ears. Apparently their discomfort outweighs my pain.

Blocked at every turn; it hurts.

Can you understand, as I stand alone before you, knocking at locked doors?

Shrinking into that small child before your eyes, but you refuse to see me. You turn away, giving me your back as you walk from me. Not wanting to see this child left standing alone, frightened, overwhelmed by thoughts, feelings, and the reality of a child left to their own devices.

Forced to travel through grown-up parental responsibilities alone.

The pain surrounds me.

All encompassing, intensified emotions.

Shaking like a leaf in the wind, shivering with the growing coldness that penetrates from the inside out and from the outside in.

I can't remember and I want to…

CHAPTER ONE

I had so many journals while I was lost, out in the world. Sadly life on the street steals many things, journals being one of them.

All those pages - lost into the place where all thrown away things go. I lost everything.

My Childhood

I never felt as if I belonged. I always felt there was something terribly wrong. This has been my reality, off and on, for as long as I can remember.

The year was 1957. Osama bin Laden was born, ultra-sound technology was pioneered, and baby boomers were at their peak.

1957... the year I came into this world, born on the cusp. I was born on the ass-end of the bull and the beginning of the twins, birthed between daylight and nightfall, that silvery hue between darkness & light. That's when I came to be. Life unfolds ironically.

For the first three years in Cornwall, we were a family of three. It was temporary.

As a young child, one of the things I remember feeling was the tension in our home. Though I never heard any yelling or fighting, the air was thick. There was a heaviness you could cut with a knife. You know that energy you feel when you walk into a room and think: Oh shit, get me out of here! It was like that.

My folks often left me in the care of the Balazi's. They ran a boarding house. I spent a whole summer there while my mom was working out the divorce details, so I'm told. Mrs. Balazi was a kind woman, motherly looking, round in stature and long black hair streaked with grey. She wore it always in a bun with a net over it. I never saw her without an apron on. You could always find her in the kitchen.

She's the one who potty-trained me, who raised me, to a certain degree. Her husband (I don't remember him but discovered later he was a pedophile) was rarely seen. They, or should I say, SHE ran the boarding house, renting rooms to travellers, salesmen, and short-term gents. Though some were hardly what you'd call a gentleman.

I remember being in the parlor room. I was a little girl, getting little-girl attention but some of that attention was not the kind any mother would want their child to get. No real parent was ever present to say anything.

I only recall faint images of the pant fabric from various renters and the odd facial outline that stood out in my mind. One man's pants, I distinctly remember, were grey trousers and something grew and moved in those pants. He didn't let me off his lap, and he started to sweat and make quiet grunting noises. I froze, ever so silent until I was released.

I remember not being allowed to go upstairs but I was just a child and children explore, and disobey. A light shone at the bottom of the stairs then faded into darkness. The wooden staircase went half way up to a platform and then took a turn the rest of the way. The staircase passage was dark and I was afraid but I walked through the darkness towards a light at the end of the hall. It was bright sunshine flooding into the room. I was drawn towards the light, it was really beautiful. There was an old man who I think was Mr. Balazi sitting on a bed in the room at the very end of the hall. I remember he sat on the edge of the bed, in his brown flannel pants and one of those standard white undershirts men of his age used to wear. His suspenders were hanging off his shoulders and his feet barely touched the floor.

It wasn't until a million years later, in my forties, when I walked into an art deco furniture store next to the Horseshoe Tavern in Toronto that it hit me. There was a bed set. My husband saw I went white as a ghost. I wasn't sure why, but everything in me froze and my husband escorted me out. Days later, flashbacks flooded in and then I remembered the headboard. I remembered it from the angle of lying flat on my back.

I'm piecing together the fragmented memories of my past. With each new memory, things fall into place and shed some awareness as to why I am not only uneasy in the darkness, but also anxious in the light. It's a really sad place to be. I had spent quite a lot of time with the Balazi's.

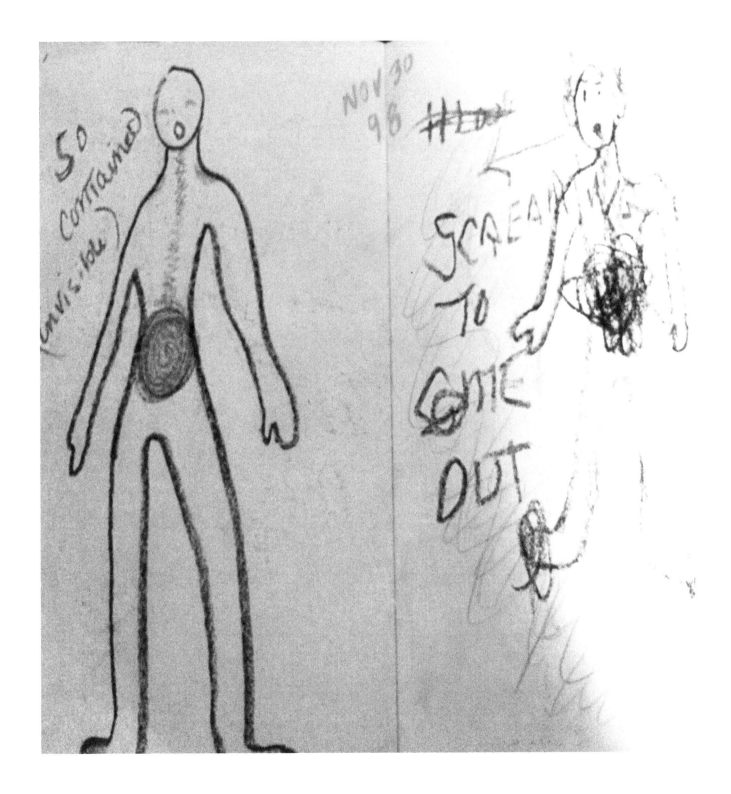

CHAPTER TWO

Divorce in the fifties was not as common as it is today. It was to become an important part of my reality. So, my mother packed up our few belongings and we boarded a train to Montreal, to stay with my Great Aunt and her family. I remember parts of the train ride. I'd lay my head on my mom's lap and she'd stroke my hair. I remember it felt comforting. My Auntie's family looked like how my family once used to be - a family of three. That image felt like salt in an open wound to me. My family was never going to be that image ever again. It was a difficult adjustment for me. So I acted out.

In one of my acting out episodes, I had cut (I think) the hair off of all of my cousin's Barbie's and if you remember that funky fabric that had the trim with the fuzzy balls... Well, I cut off all those balls too. Yes, I was probably scolded. I must say, especially to my cousin, "I'm really sorry I did that".

My father had come to visit me after my parents divorced. He brought me a doll that I really wanted, a Chatty Cathy. Actually, he bought two, one for me and one for my cousin who was two years older than me at the time. However, one of the dolls was stolen right out of his car. It was quite a mystery. I mean, who would steal a doll meant for my cousin? I got mine. I remember taking special care of my Chatty Cathy and making a little bed for her in one of my drawers but in the morning she was GONE! No one seemed to know anything and that mystery remained unsolved for many years.

While staying with my Great Aunt, I had a birthday party. I remember all these kids I didn't know showed up to my party on the apartment building's grounds. There was even a clown. I hate clowns! I was expected to be a little hostess, like being groomed for my womanly duties in life. The wind was blowing, paper plates were flying. As I ran around on my own trying to collect them, I caught a glimpse of a beautiful majestic weeping willow tree. I was drawn in, as if we had a deep embedded connection. She was a magnificent tree. Her weeping branches would bend and sway, as if dancing in the wind. She penetrated my heart and mesmerized me.

So many disjointed memories - good mixed with strange.

After staying with my Great Aunt, we moved into our own one-bedroom apartment in Montreal on Sherbrooke Street, apartment #103. The superintendents, Mr. and Mrs.

Beaupre, were a seemingly caring couple who had no children of their own. They took me under their wing.

It was deep in the basement of this apartment building where he did what he pleased with me and nothing good ever came from any of it.

In that basement, no one sees the dirty little secrets that took place.

The truth is, there had been sexual abuse even before Montreal, before the age of three. Flashes of memories triggered by various things such as smells and objects if you know what I mean.

Before my parent's divorce and before we left Cornwall, there had already been sexual abuse. I remember I told the wife of the man who touched me. She and her husband were friends of my parents. I remember her name was Dodi and after I said something about it to her, she went around telling all the adults I was a liar and not to be believed. I discovered this later in life and can't help but shake my head. I was barely three years old. Who does that? Who blames the victim and stands by her man when a toddler makes such a claim? My scars deepened further. They would last a lifetime.

In the fifties and sixties big brooms swept everything away. Everything was hush- hush back then. It was the "Leave it to Beaver" era, picture perfect images of picture perfect families. Far from the reality of many folks, but this is what one presented to the world back then or at least tried to.

My foundation was broken and lay crumbled before me, making it difficult to build anything upon it. I wasn't able, at that tender age, to understand or make sense of any of it. But, I felt it all. I slid down the rabbit hole in a panic, frozen in time, fucked-up in my mind.

My mother eventually got a job with a talent agency in Montreal and put me into a French Catholic boarding school. I was the only English Jew there. I did not mesh well into the mainstream. I always felt like an outsider looking in and played mostly on my own. I lived at the school during the week and came home on weekends, where the Beaupre's often took care of me.

Mrs. Beaupre taught me how to roll her cigarettes and Mr. Beaupre took me to the basement.

He not only sexually abused me on a weekly basis, but he also rented me out to his buddies.

Deep in the basement where no one sees, wooden slat lockers lined the walls. The smell of mothballs, dampness, and dust filled the air from the ground to the ceiling. Dim lights pushed in between the old wooden slats. I could see dust particles floating in the air. It's what I focused on when he did it. He was a big man, or maybe he just seemed big to me because I was little and he stood over me.

My panties down, my dress lifted up around my neck, his large hands touching me. I remember men waiting their turn.

The reality was I was being trafficked. Though it was not until 2019 when I came to that awareness. Back then, there was no word to describe those secret things that were happening to me. As recovery and healing takes place, more details always get revealed. Like peeling an onion it makes me cry with each new layer. Getting to the core can be heartbreaking.

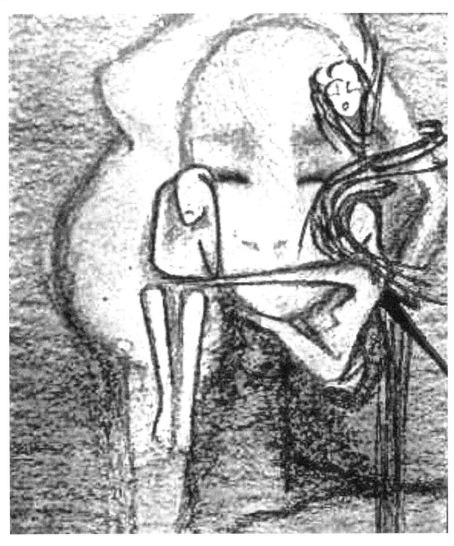

I think I remember that moment of disassociation.

It was like a giant strip of Velcro being torn apart. You know that loud ripping sound it makes when you tear the two pieces apart? It was just like that, but happening inside my body, mind and spirit at the same time.

I disconnected from myself and everything else around me.

Life went on but I was frozen in time. I was living life in full pantomime and building a giant wall around myself.

I was surrounded by an emotional disconnect, as if I had been hatched or dropped into this world. I was unable to bond. A huge black, bottomless pit grew huge inside me as I craved to fill it in or run away and avoid it all together. Filling and avoiding that hole inside me became the sole function of my life.

I knew instinctively as a child something was very wrong but I lacked the vocabulary to articulate it and grew up in an era when silence was considered golden. No one wanted to know. No one wanted to see what was happening to me. What was I going to say? I didn't even have the vocabulary to try.

I just closed my eyes.

Out of sight... out of mind is how it's supposed to be... or so I was lead to believe. That really didn't work for me.

Not having the words or ability to express what happened to me didn't change as I got older. I just didn't have the tools I needed in my teens or a large portion of my grown up years for that matter. I really had no ability to speak. My voice had been silenced.

So much shame and trauma had permeated my being. I was unable to contain what was stirring in me. My acting out was a result of an explosion of instances of not being heard. My childhood and my voice had been stolen. I was unable to tell my own story. I was broken emotionally, spiritually, intellectually, and physically.

My mother was in a new relationship. His name was Bud. I don't remember him ever touching me inappropriately but he was a jealous man. He got jealous if my mother paid too much attention to me. Every week he would buy me a chocolate bar and as a kid, I thought that was sweet. I also remember going on weekend drives together and I think he made it possible for my mom and I to go on outings. However, many times the energy was yucky. I don't think my mom was terribly happy with Bud. Once I recall thinking it was as if he was a Kleenex. You know, you blow your nose in it and toss it away, but yet he was still there every day.

I hated that apartment in Montreal.

Mrs. Beaupre caught her husband with his hands down my pants when I was in my tweens. This woman, who had taught me how to roll her cigarettes and had played a quasi, mother role to me, now lashed out and blamed me for her husband's actions. She threw me out. She yelled terrible things at me. I was crushed.

Mrs. Beaupre never told my mother what she saw and I had been trained to keep the secrets and remain silent. I was told by Mr. Beaupre long ago that what he did to me was a secret and that bad things would happen if I told my mother. He said we would be out on the street if anyone found out.

It's that I'm afraid what people will think
my own judgment — what will people think
what do I think

CHAPTER THREE

One day my mother fell in love with another man. He was an American Navy man. Tom. The asshole!

We moved from our little one-bedroom apartment in Montreal to a small house in Hopewell, Virginia.

I had my very own room, away from Mr. Beaupre, my basement abuser. Finally!

I had never lived in a house before, let alone have my very own room. Tom even got me a record player, it was all mine. I listened to Jesus Christ Superstar over and over. Tom used to give me money "to go play in traffic" as he used to say in a joking manner. I think he really meant it though.

I eventually started to not like Tom and I don't think he liked me all that much either. The town of Hopewell was so beautiful to look at. It was just like a postcard until you took a closer look.

There was a white section and a black section, and God help you if you crossed over the line. At night you could hear the screams. Later I learned the word 'lynching.'

Every weekend Tom and his two friends, a woman who was incredibly large with pink eyes (she looked like a giant rat) and a fellow who was the size of a tall toothpick would drink. That's pretty much all they did. Drink! Every weekend!

Things started to unravel. My mother was really not happy again with Tom and called her ex-boyfriend. He would come to rescue us but while we packed and waited for him the shit had already hit the fan. Tom was no longer drinking with his friends. They were now driving by in his pickup truck, firing shotguns, yelling profanity out the windows and my mom and I shivered in fear inside what was now an empty house with old white sheets pinned up over the windows. We had a few cans of Campbell's soup, a small warped aluminum pot and a glass container of coffee. It was during this time I saw my Mom grasping at a bottle holding onto it for dear life. I witnessed my mother fall apart before my eyes, without her uttering a word to me. I witnessed it all, and we both remained silent throughout because that's how it's done.

Bud, my mother's ex from Montreal eventually arrived and as we were escaping into his car, my cat jumped out of my arms. The grown-ups said "Leave it! We don't have time to retrieve a damn cat". I was devastated.

We headed for a cheap motel in Florida. I don't remember much about our drive. My mother was most likely very distraught. I barely remember seeing her and I so desperately needed to be comforted for all that happened. So, I found comfort in the arms of a motel guest whose name I don't even remember. He was 23 years old. I was just 13 years old.

CHAPTER FOUR

Without any discussion, I was put on a plane and sent back to Canada to go live with my father in Niagara Falls and his new replacement family. I found out that my father and his new family didn't know I was even coming until I was already halfway there.

Once back in Canada, I remember feeling so very small inside the airport because everything seemed very large and overwhelming to me. It was much like a scene from Alice in Wonderland. It was surreal. Once we arrived at his house, I was given the message to fit in and make like I belonged. I was always expected to behave as if nothing out of the ordinary had ever happened to me. I was to blend in. When I was unable to comply I was blamed for being bad. I internalized all of it.

Mixed Messages flooded in.

Of course as I approached my teens, like any teen, rebellion was par for the course. It was a right of passage. Having left a number of non-kosher, perverted situations and carrying the heavy bags of my past experiences along with me with no understanding or protective grown-ups present, everything just kind of exploded.

Molly, my very first best friend suddenly died of meningitis. I was devastated yet I do not remember any words of comfort coming my way from anyone. I recall feeling as if I was supposed to act the way they wanted me to, like nothing terrible had just happened. Truth is, I did act normal considering the circumstances.

They didn't see it that way at all. Ever!

It is sad how blind people can be.

I was just 14 years old when I developed a crush on one of my other friend's older brothers.

He raped me.

I got home past curfew and remember my step-mother slapped my face. She shamed me and called me a slut.

I hadn't realized my shirt was on inside out and she jumped to conclusions before even asking me why I was late. The sad truth about this instance was I was more distraught at the thought of being late for curfew than being raped.

At times, my father would threaten to disown me and I was always being compared to my younger half-sister who was the apple of their eyes. It was very clear that I fell short of being an acceptable human being that they would want to have in their family. I knew they were stuck with me and I felt what that meant every day.

In my childhood, I was always being sent away. I always felt unwanted. Mom sending me to Dad and Dad sending me back to Mom every summer. I once overheard their conversation. It went something like this "We'd want her to stay if she was just different than who she is."

Who the fuck says shit like that, I mean really.

My teen years were hell but then again so was my stolen childhood. There was nothing innocent about those years.

I wanted to be seen so badly but at the same time I also wanted to disappear and be invisible because those who saw me, saw me in a sexual way or as someone who was never good enough. I just never measured up to anyone's expectations.

Shortly after moving to Niagara Falls with my Dad and the family who didn't want me, I attempted suicide and ended up in the psychiatric ward.

I remember my parents berating me for not complying with the psychiatrist, whose opening line was "What's your problem today? Drop your pants young lady." My parents gave me shit for not doing as the doctor told me to. He had labeled me as a non-compliant, uncooperative patient.

If only they knew. If only they had bothered to ask me or even tried to talk to me. I doubt I would have said anything. But they didn't even try. It was not the kind of relationship we had. Anything I had to say was of no value to them. I just didn't fit into their lives. I was baggage dumped on them which was obviously an uncomfortable, unwelcome situation for them.

If only... if only.

It is what it is. I learned to cope to the best of my ability.

It's common to send kids of divorced families back and forth between parents and families but for me I just always felt as if I was being sent away. To some it may not seem like a big deal, but it was to me, It hurt.

I think when kids go back and forth between divorced parents it is so both parents can spend time with their child. The format still exists today but my time with my mother was so limited because I lived in a French Catholic boarding school and when I was sent back to my father, he was barely around. I certainly never got to spend time with him unless it was to be scolded, talked to, or lectured.

I knew there were many hard financial times, as my dad couldn't support both families, and the new family always took priority. I got to watch and hear about all the stuff I didn't get to experience. I was supposedly part of his family but I didn't get new bikes, go on trips or enjoy camp adventures like my siblings did. This continued for a lifetime. Pass the salt so the wound can burn just a tad more.

I had no real connection to my siblings. The whole thing was really fucking weird. Honestly, I had no connection to anybody, anywhere.

As an adult, I can't help but shake my head and wonder what the hell they were thinking. I must have drawn the short straw. I was unlucky with both parents.

Holy shit! As I'm writing this I feel like Cinder-fucking-rella.

I had been schooled in French so I was way behind when I was shipped off to my father's house and went to English public school. I had been taught the metric system. I didn't know how many inches were in a foot. Everything and everyone left me feeling as if I was stupid but the worst was getting that message from my parents. Their lack of understanding still boggles my mind.

Blame the victim. It never occurred to anyone to look beyond the surface. My acting out and suicide attempts never seemed to cause anyone much concern. I was a source of aggravation.

Actually, I found out years later that my stepmother suspected that something had happened or was happening to me in my childhood but she, nor my Dad certainly didn't do anything about it. They just continued along their way blaming me for not being 'normal.'

I was normal. Very normal considering what I was surviving.

I stayed in Niagara Falls for about three years. That was as much as I could handle. After the death of my friend Molly and being in a place I didn't feel wanted and knew I didn't belong, I left.

I overheard many discussions between my father and stepmother about how they wished I wasn't there and some real nasty stuff about my mother. They said they couldn't put me in foster care. That wasn't an option they would consider. Maybe it was because of what people would think. Honestly, I don't know.

I was a pain in their ass just by my presence. I just couldn't fit in anywhere and I couldn't pretend that what had happened to me never happened. The problem was I couldn't voice any of it.

I left Niagara Falls without a dime in my pocket. The only thing I knew was I was heading back to Montreal. Somehow!

I did not sneak out in the middle of the night. I spoke with my parents who seemed both angry and thrilled I was leaving. They had no concern about leaving without any money, having no address to go to and they had absolutely no concern about my safety. When you think about it, they really hadn't been concerned about anything concerning me up to this point, so why would that change now? Or maybe they just didn't know how to show concern to a kid like me. My father did threaten to disown me if I left. The last words I remember him saying were "You have no family. Thank God you're leaving and Get out!" I wasn't even sixteen years old at the time.

CHAPTER FIVE

I hitchhiked back to Montreal. I sat hungry and cold in a hotel lobby trying my best to get a paid date to prostitute myself. I had no idea what I was doing. I didn't know how to do this myself as it had always been done to me. After all, I'd been a commodity since early childhood.

Finally a man approached me and invited me up to his room. I was so naïve. I went into the bathroom to disrobe and came out with a towel wrapped around me.

There was a stern knock on the door.

"Police!... Open up!"

I was arrested and sent to juvenile hall. To the best of my knowledge, nothing happened to the man who had engaged me as a minor! I was terrified of them calling my father, which they did.

He drove all the way from Niagara Falls to the police station to tell me he was leaving me there in Montreal and what a shameful, disgusting human being I was. He laid the shame on so thick it's taken me years to wash it off.

Those scars are still present today and visible, depending on your ability to see.

I learned a lot in juvenile detention. I served my time. While there, not one counselor counseled me. I was told the rules and expected to behave.

When I was finally released and sent back to Ontario, my father put me in the Elmwood Residence for Women in downtown Toronto because there was no way he was going to allow me back home.

At the Elmwood, they were all senior citizens in their eighties and it had that old person smell everywhere. It was dark and dingy. Basically the place was falling apart.

One old gal told me she'd been there forever and that she had been hit by lightning twice sitting in her room. The place freaked me out.

I got a job in a leather shop but the owner wouldn't cash my cheque unless I bought something. My cheque didn't cover the cost of anything in the shop and I had to pay rent in the hellhole I was put in. Tears rolled down my face.

One of the regular shoppers, who I had gotten chummy with, came in and saw me crying. She asked me if I wanted to move in with her and one other girl down on McGee Street. She could even help me get a job where she worked in a massage parlor. I had to get out of the situation I was in so I took her up on her offer.

One thing lead to another, with each decision I made, the further I was becoming immersed in an underworld society. I started working in various massage parlors in Toronto where everyone took their cut. There was absolutely no safety anywhere to be found. I was running from one scary situation into the next.

I returned to Montreal and continued to work. I basically was a working, walking commodity everywhere and anywhere. It didn't matter if I was getting groceries, if an opportunity presented itself I took it. You'd be surprised how many dates came as a result of grocery shopping. In fact, one store became a part of my stroll.

Working the streets was pretty much all I knew and I had grown up believing I was merchandise. Working independently was not often an option and it became pretty risky.

My life is somewhat blurry. I don't remember what came first. The order of things in my mind is messed up and chronologically out of place at times. It's a nightmare in my mind and causes me much anxiety.

My family back then would never believe me if I couldn't recall the order of things because they assumed I was making up stories. It was a time when I had to prove everything I did or said as if there were witnesses that would come forward to dispute my statements. Back then, if a girl's skirt was too short, she was asking for it and rape and violence was not even questioned if you were a girl like me, working the streets.

We were considered subhuman and prostitutes can't get raped. No one took us seriously. It wasn't even worth it to bother reporting those instances to police. What a joke!

While I was working the streets some of the jail-keepers and cops were okay. Sometimes, it was like a game for me to out run them so I could continue working. If I got caught, I did an overnighter in jail and then was released. I got to know the cops on the beat, the gatekeepers, the staff working the jail and the morality squad. Moral my ass! I can't even begin to tell you how many blow jobs I gave in order not to be jailed overnight.

I'm truly sorry my story is this heavy and not neatly packaged but I'm not neatly packaged either.

CHAPTER SIX

I know my first drug injection took place in Toronto at Larry's Hideaway.

I was terribly afraid of needles but a guy I had met kept offering, kept pushing and one day I gave in. I extended my arm and looked the other way. As the drug entered my bloodstream, heat crept through my body. I was instantly hooked.

He wanted to fuck me but I wanted to dance and luckily I left in one piece and danced the night away as the drug coursed through my body and my mind calmed down. I was hooked. From that very first time, I had found the perfect escape.

I don't remember the year or how old I was exactly. I was probably only 17 or 18 at the time. I remember because Misses Night at the Domino Club on Isabella Street had just opened. My mother had returned to Toronto and I was able to live with her in her apartment in a building on Eglinton Avenue. The building has now been converted into a senior's residence.

This goes back in time to before the second subway stop on Eglinton West even existed.

This was around the time the mystery of the Chatty Cathy doll was finally solved. My mom told me she had stolen both Chatty Cathy dolls because she told my father not to buy them and he went ahead and bought them anyway. For so long it was such a mystery to me and when I heard that it was my mom who took my doll I was in shock. So much pain had accumulated in my life to this point but the lesson I learned that day was that if my mother could do that to me, her very own baby girl, then anyone and everyone was able to screw me over and hurt me.

No one was to be trusted, No one. My heart ached to feel safe with someone, anyone. I was motivated by pure desperation to feel a connection. I hated feeling so alone.

I stayed with my mother only for a short time and it was during that time when I met a handsome fella who lived in our building.

I started spending time with him. He gave me small gifts and treated me well. He gave me the attention I was so desperate for but he was grooming me.

Without knowing it, I had hooked up with a pimp with violent tendencies and I was now his property. I now had an owner. I worked and worked and worked. I kept none of the money.

Eventually I ran, like I had always done before. I said nothing to my mom. It seemed my life was either running away or being sent away.

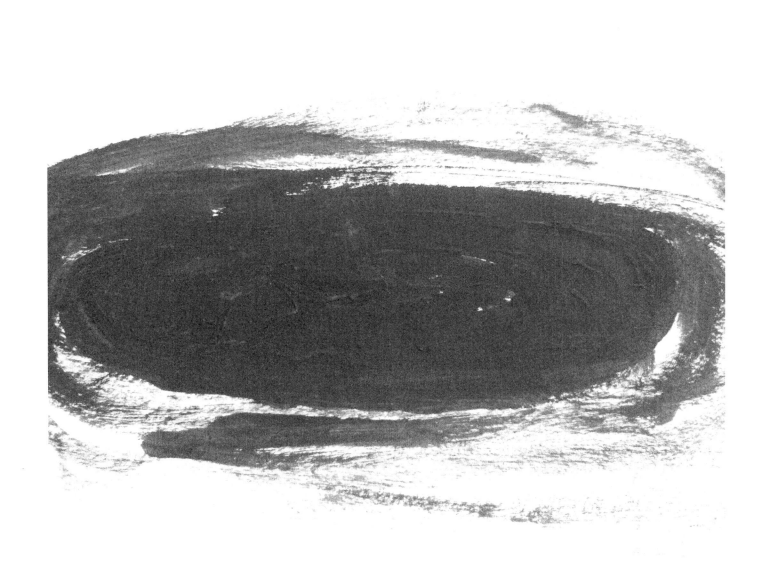

CHAPTER SEVEN

Back in Montreal I hit the streets again. I went from one pimp to the next being groomed and taken advantage of. There was an in-between courting time that all pimps seem to know about or more accurately a poaching time that gives a girl a short few days rest to catch her breath before she is put to work again.

If you've made it this far in my story, good for you, as I am aware this is heavy stuff, though I can't help but think, Wow! This heavy stuff is what I carried as a child. Sad indeed, but I do want to let you know there is light at the end of the tunnel. Things did get better, but for now, let's plow through the dark to get to the light.

Much of my past is a blur. Some might say it's because of the drugs, but I'd say it's because of the trauma. In all its complexity, trauma had a bigger impact on me than any drug ever could. The lack of protection I felt was the most debilitating part of my life back then. Recently, I found out that trauma often rewires everything in your body including the nervous system. So yeah, that was me.

I still, to this day, struggle to stay connected to myself. Pretending and going through the motions of life is no way to live.

I was desperate for what was missing in my life, to feel protected and loved. I longed to feel a part of something. I yearned for a sense of belonging but most importantly to be believed. The ache was so deep and painful that it drove my very existence. I had no map or stable influence to guide me. No one to turn to that could help me find my way out. I didn't even have the vocabulary to express my feelings. I was trying to build a life with no tools and even as I grew, my ability to express myself was damaged. I thought I was beyond repair until I hit my mid-30s. Half my life I spent being dazed and confused, lost and bewildered.

Addiction was a natural diversion. Surprise! I would use anything to escape and just get through a moment in time. Being in my body and soberly present was never an option for me back then. I still struggle with that today but not as intensely.

My family, friends, and the world pointed fingers in a re-victimization fashion as if using was a choice. It was a survival mechanism that worked. Even if it was just temporarily it offered relief. Over time however, the damage and harm I had accumulated along the way took its toll. I just wanted to not feel the intensity of pain inside me. It was like having open heart surgery without anesthetic. Tearing flesh. Shredding emotions. It was sheer and utter Hell.

To top it off, my parents constantly reminding me of how fucked up I was sure didn't help. It was more salt being rubbed in an already hemorrhaging wound.

With addiction came a whole slew of other issues and ugliness. I saw so many horrors as I travelled the underbelly of society. So many things I still cannot unsee. These images still rear their ugly heads from time to time. I am always baffled when people sometimes ask me, "Why are you sad?" I never know how to answer that question. I have a million reasons as to why I feel sad or triggered. Pick one. Any one will do.

I remember when I was an active IV drug user I gathered water out of a street puddle to drink or to clean something and the woman I was with went partially blind doing the same thing. I later learned it was the street water that had affected her sight. I don't know why my sight wasn't lost or damaged as hers was. A little blessing in a dark time I guess.

I was falling deeper into that deep, dark pit. It had become part of my DNA. To some degree I think I was born inside that pit and kept sliding deeper into the depths of its despair...

WHY BE
I needed too

EMPOWERMENT

EM POWERMENT

Be yourself

What does it all mean?

ARE U?

WHO

Tell us
what
you
want
to BE!

Be yourself

CHAPTER EIGHT

The sale of girls, boys, and infants was commonplace back then and sadly still is now. It used to be called slavery. Now we call it human trafficking. The younger the victim, the higher the price would be. Pimps would treat their stables to furs and treats. It's really tricks for treats but that's something you would never say out loud. No one wanted to admit they were paying for love.

The johns pay for sex.

The working girls pay for protection. Of course there really was no protection of any real consequence. What a joke!

And we paid for what we thought was love or the illusion of being loved. No loving person who truly loves you would ever ask you to do such things.

The world would pass its judgment as if these women, including me, were less than human, like we were undeserving of decency. The truth is, we were all damaged and desperate to be loved and protected. This was the way it was. This was the way it had to be in order to survive.

Time stood still for me back then. No longer did it matter what day it was, what week it was, or what year it was. It all came together like a mudslide.

With sexual abuse, neglect, and human trafficking came addiction and mental health issues. It all impacted me physically.

With addiction came street life. With street life came more addiction, more sex trade and more human trafficking.

It all came with the rotation of holding tanks, jail cells and punishment. It was physical, emotional and spiritual scabs that never healed. I felt constantly unsafe and exposed to the underbelly of street life in the city.

In Montreal, women would try to befriend me and bring me over to their pimps promising stability, collecting brownie points while climbing some weird fucked-up ladder. It's not safe to be independent and on the streets at least not for any length of time. I could on and on with what seems like never-ending barrage of bad anecdotes about life on the street.

I worked everywhere at all times of the day or night. In the morning I'd catch johns on their way to work and then the lunch crowd shortly after. Then came happy hour and the midnight strollers, finally! My favourite was the morning run because dates were quick. They had to be. They couldn't be late for work.

It was a blur.

And then one day, I was trafficked over the border to the United States. Human trafficking like I had really never experienced. I vaguely remember how it even happened.

It was around 3am. I was leaving a bar somewhere in Montreal. I had no specific plans and just jumped into a car and hit the road with a bunch of strangers that I so easily and mistakenly called friends back then. Probably folks I had just met. I don't even remember their names. They drove me to Miami.

Once there, we all seemed to go our separate ways but I found myself alone. As I walked around in God knows what area, I met some fellows. They flirted with me and I hung with them. Then they invited me to a house party that turned into a hellish scene out of a bad movie. It took me a while to comprehend the fact I was now trapped on foreign soil.

The guys I came to the party with had disappeared after introducing me to another fellow and it wasn't until I went to leave that I realized the severity of the situation. This was my introduction to a more hardcore form of human trafficking with very little grooming. It was more like a bang and heroin game. I had indulged in all kinds of drugs to this point but heroin was always something I stayed away from. That was a drug of no return.

Ironically, looking back now, I could say being introduced to heroin initially had been my saving grace because I don't think I would have survived being stuffed in the trunk of a car had I not been so high from the drug. Reality hit me. I had just been sold to another guy at the party.

Stashed away with a few other women, I started to understand the gravity of my predicament. I was not the youngest nor was I the oldest and some of the girls looked like they had been there for quite some time. The elders had a blank deadness in their eyes. The newbies had fear in theirs.

The initial goal of our captors was to break our spirits. Some were in charge of keeping the 'herd' in line and the violence was extreme. You really had to watch your every move. The pecking order was as brutal as anything you could imagine but no one was allowed to hit your face. No visible scars or markings as it lowered your price. The ones who had been there for a long time and were no longer profitable simply disappeared.

Those who tried to escape often vanished and were never to be seen again. We never thought it was because they got sent home. That's just not how things worked. They could have been re-sold, passed from one trafficker to the next as a commodity, or used to pay off debts or return favours. Some I am sure were possibly buried six feet deep. Who the hell knows?!

Discipline was always handed out in front of us all to make a point. It was meant to strike the fear of God in us, right down to our bones. It's not like we were privy to any valuable information. Initially we were handcuffed to pipes or beds or put in cages. We were intimidated until fear set in so deep that escape was no longer an option.

My human trafficking nightmare began in Florida but I was transported across state lines sometimes in the trunk of cars to states I cannot even venture to tell you. It's not like we got to visit anywhere and see sites. Every state, every place all looked like the last dark and dingy room.

I remember there was a young girl who clung to me. I found comfort in that human, emotional connection, even if it was sheer terror she was feeling. (I need to stop and dry my eyes as I reflect on that time.)

She's gone, probably, forever. Even if that little girl survived, she will never be the same. None of us will. What they did to her cannot be undone. What I witnessed can't be unseen. That's my reality.

Once, I heard the sound of an electric sander. I smelled burnt flesh. The screams continue to echo in my being to this day.

Days turned into nights, nights turned back into days. Over and over, it all seemed like one long continuous blending of light and darkness in a perpetual loop. Men pawing at me, coming inside of me and sweating on top of me…. Day in and day out.

Once when I was in the trunk, I remember vaguely hearing the sound of muffled voices coming from inside the car. I remember laying very still and wondering if I was going to end up buried deep in some back wood forest or found dead in a dumpster in some city. I tried not to breath. I feared running out of air but that didn't happen to me.

I don't remember how I eventually got away. I tried to run away in the beginning but learned quickly the price one pays for that transgression. I have no idea how long I was trapped there in the grips of human trafficking. I had lost my grasp on pretty much everything. I knew no one was even looking for me. Certainly no one in from my family cared enough to notice I was gone and I had no friends or trusted confidante. I had nobody.

I venture to say that in the first 30 years of my life I was a victim of human trafficking. I had many owners along the way but it was all the same crap. I belonged to someone as a sexual object.

It is still a mystery to me how I ended up on a bus back to Canada. I honestly have no idea how that went down. I guess I'll toss it in the pile of missing pieces that I've been collecting along the way.

All I know is I was on a bus. I don't recall much of the ride but I do know I left with the clothes on my back and a little bit of money. Customs never even questioned me. Crossing the border back then, no passports were required.

Upon my return to Canada, I went right back to working the streets. After all, what else was I going to do? And now I had a drug habit to support. Otherwise I would get sick from withdrawals and not be able to work. Back then the support systems for people like me didn't exist.

I had escaped my American traffickers but I had to be made an example of. I couldn't be the one that got away. That news travelled across borders despite having no internet back then. Once I was back on the streets of Montreal, the pimp I initially ran away from when I took the ride to the United States, beat me beyond recognition.

deserve
PLEASE STAND BY
SHUT UP
Be yourself
Behold.
ATTENTION
The times they are a changin'.
One of a Kind
Refuse to blend.
my soul,
Blurred vision
PRICELESS
The Only Piece Missing Is You
part of me
here forever.
Shutout
TIME
different ?

There is a line one crosses when a violent beating becomes so intense that pain is no longer felt. It doesn't matter anymore. Not even the fear of being left for dead matters. You just surrender. I remember boots and crowbars kicking and hitting me on my arms and legs. My body was beaten like I had never been beaten before. Even my face was a mess of broken bones and bruises.

I laid on the floor in the fetal position, shivering and broken. Beatings became the norm. Though I had escaped human trafficking, the scars of that time in my life still remain and I'm left to deal with them to this day.

CHAPTER NINE

Let's take a breather.

I know I need one right about now.

I am aware this is not the lightest of subjects, to say the least. I eventually healed my external scars but going back to the streets triggered a new panic for me, especially after the last beating I endured.

I had turned to a fellow I barely knew. He had once barred me from his club some time ago for smoking a joint in the bathroom. I barged into his office with my hands over my broken face and burst into tears. He took me to his home, told me I'd be safe, left me alone and returned to work. He took care of me. In that I found some comfort. But I was a junkie. I needed a fix.

As I began to get sick, he locked me in a room for about three weeks. I quit cold turkey. I got off the junk. Our relationship grew. No one had ever extended a hand like that to me before. It shifted into a business relationship of sorts. It was another grooming. Here we go again. But he was non-violent. By this time I didn't even need to be groomed. I just knew what was expected of me. I stayed with him for five years. Yes, I continued to work but I was now off the streets... but a trick is a trick. When you grow up feeling like a commodity, it is the natural order of things.

After about three weeks of getting sick in order to get clean, I got antsy. I had to work at pretty much the only thing I knew how to do, so he connected me to a few brothels in order to keep me off the streets but still I was a money making machine.

I know this may sound weird but I felt safe working in brothels, such as the famous Mustang Ranch brothel in Reno, Nevada. I also worked a lot for Ada McCallum, who ran a brothel in Halifax. You could say I grew up there.

Working there I was kept away from the bullshit of street life. There I was drug-free. I had to be. I got into a routine and that was good for me. Still, I was a commodity.

I remember the first time I arrived at the Mustang Ranch. There was red velvet everywhere and a series of paintings depicting a story out of the old west during the saloon days. In one painting women were decked out in bustle dresses and fancy hats as they carried the casket of one of their own to the grave. Although I felt trapped in a 'future' scene of that painting heading to my own demise, I somehow survived.

At the Mustang Ranch, each of our rooms was connected to a shared washroom and there was a panic button in every room. Here's how it worked. A bell would ring and we would line up. The hostess brought a man into the main hall where we'd say our names and nothing more. He would be asked to pick one of us and if he couldn't, he would then go to the bar. We would all tag along to chat him up while trying to seal the deal.

We never left Mustang Ranch, everything was brought in. They supplied us with lingerie, clothes and jewelry. Even hairdressers would be brought in! We never left. There was a man who was responsible for handling and depositing our earnings once a week. We trusted him, he was bonded. We worked three weeks on and one week off.

You had to be medically pre-screened before you were even allowed to start working at the Ranch. The fee back then was $150. Then you were brought to Carson City where you had to go to the Marshall's office to get your license to work. That was another $25. Funny the things you remember.

Joe Conforte, who ran the Ranch, decided once to take his top girls off to see the boxing fights at a casino in Reno, Nevada. I got to go as I had often bedded Joe and I did like his bodyguard very much. He was a big, tall man with a gentle disposition, at least with me he was. His name was Lucky. On the day of the fight, I went into my room and found a beautiful gown lying on the bed. And jewelry (lots of bling), high heels, and a fur coat (remember we were in the desert). It really felt as if I had entered a B movie. We got dressed up and all piled into a big stretch limousine and drove from the desert into Reno. When we entered the casino, the crowd parted and the whispers were clear to hear. Guests muttered things like, 'Those are Joe's girls.'

The attitude at the Ranch was different than on the streets. Maybe it's because prostitution was legal but I didn't feel as if the clients there looked at us as lesser-than. In all honesty, we could have been secretaries. It was like that. And a client who showed up for the first time usually looked like a deer caught in headlights.

From that point on I travelled from brothel to brothel. Funny to think of a whorehouse as a safe place but not all of them offered the same degree of safety. Meanwhile, when not working in brothels, I was still using a variety of other drugs and still lived a life removed from society's norm. While working in brothels, I was pretty much drug-free.

When I worked in Halifax for Ada McCallum, our hours were from 3pm to 5am, six days a week. On Sundays, we got to start at 5pm and go to 5am. While there, the girls and I shared two apartments with four women in each unit. Ada took half the earnings and the hours were long but the money was good.

Ada McCallum was considered a class act and owned pretty much everyone in Halifax. Over the years, she and I shared many, many cups of tea. She was somewhat motherly to us and well-loved by all. Except when she'd send us to a place we really didn't want to go or we thought unsafe. I guess she had the attitude that no one would fuck with her and her girls. I wished that was true but it wasn't. As I remember, I experienced a few beatings and some close calls.

A couple of hoodlums broke into her house once when she was an elderly lady living in Dartmouth. They had tied her to a chair but she did manage to get free. She was a spunky lady! The guilty parties were eventually found with cement shoes. Police patrolled the-neighborhood regularly to make sure she was safe. Ada had a lot of pull with the police as well as upper society.

It's a vicious cycle. A trick for a trick, nothing changed. Pimps who gave their girls gifts were looked at so wonderfully but gifts like jewelry, fur coats and such were often used as a poaching tools when other pimps would try to convince a gal to jump ship. The truth is, whatever gifts we received, we paid for them ten times over. We paid dearly.

Eventually I ended up homeless for a number of years like the gals you'd see on Barton Street in Hamilton, Ontario. For me it was Sherbourne Street and the Parkdale area in downtown Toronto. I was now feeding a crack habit but was mostly I was a mainliner if I could find a vein.

CHAPTER TEN

Well, we are now going to shift-toward the lighter stuff.

The shift from victim to survivor.

At 34 years of age I entered rehab.

By that time I was, and had been, homeless for a number of years. No longer trafficked but every dime went into my veins. I remember one bad date in the bushes. He shoved my face into the dirt and another one who tried to drown me down at Cherry Beach. I lived in stairwells and dark corners. One time, I lived in a stranger's Mercedes that was parked in some underground lot in Parkdale. When I found shelter it always came at a cost. I was on the road to becoming a bag lady. I had been on the street surviving on my own. Winter was approaching and I didn't think I would last another winter on the street. I met a guy who was kind to me and helped me out of a few jams. We developed a relationship, though strings were always attached. He was still kind and relatively safe. Then I was headhunted. It was a thing back then. Headhunters got paid to find dissolute addicts and arrange to send them to treatment in the United States that our Canadian government would pay for. So off I went to Houston, Texas for 33 days of rehab.

This was when things shifted drastically for me.

Some interesting and motivating factors happened while I was in Texas. I met some really cool people. There was a young boy, about 18, who had already been to a number of drug treatment centres. He rarely spoke but when he did, he always had something of substance to say. I couldn't help but think, he's a kid, I'm an adult woman and what the hell does he know?

Turning point! I realized if he can do it, fuck it, I can, too. I had so much to release and so many silent screams lay dormant in me. I was also the only female in the ward. One fella tried to get with me with bribes of chocolate bars. (If you could see me, you would see my eyes rolling on that one). There was this one big man from Detroit that I became close with because I called him on his bullshit in group one day. I remember my knees were knocking together, as this was a scary thing to do but somebody had to do it. I sat silently for a while, hoping someone else in the group would step up and do it but nada, nothing. So I took a chance. Even though I knew everyone in the group, including the facilitator, wouldn't be able to hold this fella back if he lunged at me. It worked out. He and I became close friends. I knew from that point on he had my back. He often asked if I wanted him to handle any other fella's improprieties. I said "No" but that I needed him to be there for me, to have my back. Trust was slowly and silently being built.

One time, we were watching the movie 'Nuts' with Barbra Streisand and it was a trigger for me. For those who don't know the movie, Streisand plays a high-end call girl who ends up murdering a client while he's in her tub. While her sanity is being assessed in court, with her parents present, it comes out that her father had regularly sexually abused her in the bath when she was a child. Triggers!!!! I could sense the others keeping an eye on me.

After the movie, we had a group and as with most groups, you have a check-in and we had the option of not participating. I decided to participate. For this group, the exercise was held outside in a large sandbox that was used for volleyball. We were going to be blindfolded. There was a large rope laid on the ground that we had to find. We had to wander through the sandbox and by only hearing the voices of those participating, not run into each other. I truly expected someone to cop a feel, using the excuse that he couldn't see. Remember, I was the only woman in the group. Despite all that, I've got to tell you, not one fella touched me. In fact, I could sense they were extra careful not to, despite us all being blindfolded.

The impact of that was so profound for me. I cannot remember their names unless I look them up in my journal. I have a deep love for that group of men. I always will. As I write this memory tears fill my eyes. Oh the memories that come flooding back are bittersweet at times.

I wanted to stay in treatment longer but couldn't. My time was up.

The day I returned to Toronto, I went straight to a meeting. I knew my only job was to make sure I got to meetings. Then came the therapy and a multitude of diagnoses. Every psychiatrist seemed to add a new label onto me - Anxiety, Depression, Complex Post Traumatic Stress Disorder, Dissociative Disorder and Borderline Personality. It was a smorgasbord of psychiatric issues.

Housing was already pre-arranged for me at Ecuhomes in Parkdale. In fact, one of the homes had been transformed from a 'crack' date drop-in spot. Ironically, I was moving into the same house with the manager who once had to deal with me in the past. She became my greatest ally. She was always there for me. (I love you, Daralee for believing in me!)

Once I was back, I sought help from the Jewish Community Family Services. I went there because, to some degree, I still had that old way of thinking that they give Jews money.

With that money came a session to assess the what's what. It was there where I met Ronnee. She was a social worker and a rarity. I felt safe with her. She believed me and protected me. She listened to me and her eyes teared up as I told my story, which was foreign to me. She walked by my side and made it possible for me to own my story and that wasn't exactly easy for me. You see, when I first began sharing my story with her, I shared it as if I was a million miles removed from my own reality. It was like I was reciting someone else's story.

We worked through the 'Courage to Heal' together. We talked about everything that happened to me but I never really talked about the human trafficking aspect because back then those words didn't even exist to my knowledge. I spent about three years with Ronnee. She was a driving force in my life. She had created a safe place for me. A safe space within a tiny little concrete box down at the JCC called her office. Initially, she told me she didn't have a lot of experience working with someone like me. I was a smart-ass and thought I'd teach her. I showed up late on my next appointment with her and this short, round woman put me in my place with such ease and grace. She told me to wait in the hallway for the same time as I had been late. She glanced over her shoulder and smiled at me and I thought, oh shit, so this is how it's going to be. Our relationship was solidified and we agreed to meet once a week, on Tuesdays.

The john who had helped me get to treatment was also present upon my return and after months of meetings, he offered me a secretarial job at his company. We had an agreement was that on Tuesdays I'd leave early for my meetings with Ronnee. I remember after a week of working, I thought I should reward myself. My first thought was a rock/crack but I played the tape through and the other reward I came up with was a pair of red cowboy boots. I didn't have enough money so I requested a pay advance instead of turning a trick. I still have those boots and I still wear them.

Nothing really changed in the world with the exception of my perception. It was definitely shifting!

I remember the day the reality of my story hit me. It was like a ton of bricks. That day I took ownership of my life. My anger and rage, which originally fueled me through therapy, intense and powerful like driving a Lamborghini, was now gone. It was replaced by pain and sadness.

I was grieving so much time lost in the turmoil of surviving my life.

It was a Thursday when remember seeing a little girl about two or three and my brutal past came crashing down on top of me. The powers that be had created an opening for me. Ronnee had a cancelation. I bawled my eyes out to her as I travelled back up the Spadina line.

Ronnee walked with integrity. She was honest and real. I think most survivors have a sixth sense recognizing bullshit or text book therapy when dealing with counselors. We crave authenticity and finding those who are the 'real deal' is difficult. We shy away from it at times because feeling that authenticity can also be extremely painful.

As the years passed, she and I worked together. It was soon a time to move on. I was going back to school because I really wasn't qualified to do very much. Like many recovering addicts, I entered the field of social services. I graduated with honours and I am a Certified Life Skills Coach and an Addiction & Mental Health Counselor. Who knew I'd love being in school?

Welcome now to burn-outs, heart-ripping reminders, and feelings of frustration with the system. I will say, there is nothing quite like making a positive difference in the life of another human being.

I often found myself working with teens. It was such a great opportunity to practice delayed gratification. Like gardening, you plant a seed and hope for the best. Praying it will sprout and flourish. That's what working with teens is all about. You don't often get to witness the benefits of your nurturing. Sometimes you do but it's delayed gratification at its best. I loved working with my clients. There are few connections that would ever be as gratifying as those who crossed my path.

I remember when I first started working at this one place. One of the kids on my caseload was a cutter. He blurted out to me that whenever he feels like cutting or feels suicidal, the staff didn't know what to do so they would send him over to psych. I remember being able to relate. Together we worked out a plan. Many of the staff challenged me on it but I was grateful my supervisor understood and supported me.

One kid, once glanced at my scarred arms, looked up at me and said "rough childhood? You, too?" The connection was made. I loved those kids. I could relate to their stories. I understood them but was trapped working in a system that didn't work properly. Though it did provide safe housing, it lacked in understanding and failed at problem solving.

Childhood is the foundation of a life. Everything is built on childhood. Without that foundation, cracks occur in the walls and everything crumbles all around us. I was unaware of this reality of childhood. A child is limited in their ability to comprehend and express what should never be a reality for anyone in the first place. So, when you see someone working the streets, even if they don't have their teeth, be kind. Remember no one's dream is to grow up and work the streets. They, or should I say we, have been victimized enough.

The pain of my past has eased through the years, though it still rears its ugly head and is always with me. It is a part of who I am. They call them flashbacks and I ride them like a roller coaster, from the beginning, middle and right to the end. I remind myself when I'm able that I've already lived through it but sometimes it's just so exhausting.

CHAPTER ELEVEN

In the midst of my last social services burn-out, I met a man. I married him and I spiraled downward through the rabbit hole once again. With a little help from a 'friend' (my doctor) I ended up at Homewood Health Centre in Guelph in its trauma program. While I was doing inner-child work, I found out I was pregnant. At 42! Holy moly, I'm going to be a mom! Married, pregnant, and in a trauma program for my honeymoon! I was going to have a girl!

I grew to the size of a house. I couldn't even see my feet. People said the strangest things to me when I was pregnant, like "Oh, you get to relive your childhood." Oh my God, good grief, Hell Noooo! I was on guard every time strangers wanted to touch my belly. It seemed like a natural reaction to me.

It took 25 hours of labour for her delivery and they had to go in because she was not coming out. When they finally handed her to me, I fell in love instantly. It was a love like I had never experienced in my whole life. It was pure and holy.

I learned that it was a time for me to be a grown-up. Someone had to be. I was delighted and terrified. I didn't know if I could be a protector but I had done so much inner-child work it helped me. For instance, I was walking on Spadina when I accidentally clipped a man with her stroller. He turned around and went to kick the stroller. My kid's stroller! Ever so calmly, I put the brakes on, raised the overhead shield so my baby wouldn't see and picked him up, right off his feet. When I put him down and went along my way, the vibration of the incident began to creep in but with it came a sense of reassurance. I could totally be a protective mama bear.

As my daughter grew so many things triggered me but I knew it wasn't about me anymore. It was now all about her. I took my triggers into therapy. I so wanted to be an emotionally present mom. That sometimes was, and is, hard for me. My husband and I had totally different ideas on parenting and finances which led to our divorce. The divorce was final when my daughter was three. I had to hold it all together. Despite the fact that my parents had also divorced when I was around the same age but I was determined to do whatever it took not to go off the deep end. Custody depended on it.

Another shift was when my daughter and I moved to Hamilton from Toronto's Kensington Market. The Jewish community in Hamilton welcomed us and to some degree, held our hands throughout the transition.

In Hamilton, I blossomed into the truest sense of myself. I grew into my own skin, scars and all. All that therapy, all that personal work and growth was coming to fruition and I could see, taste, and feel it.

While my daughter was young, I stayed single as I had that nagging voice reminding me that I hadn't picked partners very well. In fact, I usually made a beeline to the worst fucker in the room. I didn't want a revolving door of men to be a part of her upbringing. I feared the impact on my daughter and on me. So, single I remained and I began to truly enjoy life as a single mother. I developed a beautiful relationship with myself, though at times it was a challenge not having help but who's to say a fella would end up being helpful anyway?

One evening, I was invited out to see Shelley's Marshall's play. "Hold Mommy's Cigarette." She connected me with Tracey Erin Smith at SOULO Theatre in Toronto. When Tracey first got in touch with me, asking if I'd like to sign up for the February workshop, my reply was "Oh no Dear, I don't do February." I did, however, sign up in March for her 10-week acting workshop. At the end of the workshop, each person had to do a 10-minute show. This is where BorderLineMe was born. I was invited to the Hamilton Fringe Festival and I won the Emerging Artist Award at the Hamilton Arts Awards. They even gave me money!

As my daughter grew up, it was towards the end of high school, I began poking around with online dating. I want to say things have changed but I never really dated before. Paid dates when I was working the streets was not real dating. Online was definitely an adventure and an eye-opening experience. Essentially, I was disillusioned by the reality. I decided, instead, to use it as a tool to practice speaking up for myself as it provided a safe space for me. So many exchanges left me feeling like a receptacle and a commodity, so I just had to speak up. I'm glad I did but no dates ever came of it.

Recently I met a man. He was renting a room from me. I spent almost a year and half getting to know him before I told him I was smitten with him. And low and behold he was smitten with me too. I am now in a happy, healthy relationship. It's finally a place where I can truly be me. It wasn't something I was looking for as I was quite happy being single but to find acceptance, a ton of laughter and a truly loving partner was all I had ever wanted. He just blew me away and still does. He has sat supportively beside me throughout the writing of my story. On some days, I'd write for a few hours then withdraw from the world, including him, for days of sleep and alone time. This book took its toll on me. He remained patient and was there for me when I emerged back into living life.

I am grateful to be able to use my experience, lost and in hell, to transform that trauma and pain into a beacon of light to help someone else through the darkness.

As of this writing, my daughter is now 19 years old and in university. She's a well-grounded young woman whom I am so damn proud of. She is my rock and my purpose for being. In my heart and in every breath I take, she is my saving grace. The journey with her has been such an honour. I am truly grateful to have her as my daughter and to be her mom.

I remember my mother sitting with me when my daughter was about 18 months old. My mom looked at me and said, "You've been a better mom to her in 18 months than I've been to you in 42 years." I was taken aback. I wanted to say it wasn't true but it was. All I said was "Thank you."

I healed the rift between my mother and me when Ronnee had asked if I'd be that hard on my mother if she were blind.

"Of course not", I said.

What Ronnee then explained to me was, "Your mother is blind, despite the fact that she can see, if you know what I mean?"

In time, our mother-daughter relationship was repaired. I learned to love and accept my mother for who she is and love her despite her shortcomings. She did the best she could with the tools she had, even though she truly sucked at early childhood parenting.

I was also taken aback and in awe of my mother's ability to own her mistakes and admit that she sucked at motherhood and failed me. As her daughter, I forgive her.

Now, I am loving my life because it's one that I never thought I'd ever have. I didn't get here alone and I want to acknowledge all those who contributed to who I am today, particularly the folks in Hamilton, Ontario. They have been a huge support system for me, so encouraging and loving. Thank you.

The road from the head to the heart can be a long journey. I want to share something I wrote a long, long time ago before I was able to speak it. A few years back, I shared it publicly. It's called "Listen".

Listen

"When I ask you to listen and you start giving advice, you have not done what I asked.

When I ask you to listen to me and you begin to tell me why I "shouldn't" feel that way, you are trampling on my feelings.

When I ask you to listen to me and you feel you have to do something to solve my problem, you have failed me, strange as that may seem.

Listen.

All I asked was that you listen, not talk or do. Just hear me.

Advice is cheap. Ten cents will get you both Dear Abby and Billy Graham in the same newspaper. That I can do for myself. I'm not helpless.

Maybe discouraged and faltering but not helpless.

When you do something for me that I can and need to do for myself, you contribute to my fear and weakness.

But when you accept as a simple fact that I do feel what I feel, no matter how irrational, then I can quit trying to convince you and get down to the business of understanding what's behind this irrational feeling. And when that's clear, the answers are obvious and I don't need advice.

Irrational feelings make sense when we understand what's behind them.

Perhaps that's why prayer works, for some people, because God is mute. He doesn't give advice or try to fix things. Just listens, and lets me work it out for myself.

So please listen and just hear me and if you want to talk, wait a minute for your turn and I will listen to you. I am not broken, damaged perhaps but not broken and it's not your place to fix me."

This story is not yet over; I have so much life still left to live. In fact, writing this book has caused other flashes, other memories and other lost parts of my life to resurface. I am currently processing those as best I can. I am making sense of them one by one and fitting them into the chronology of time, placing those pieces into the puzzle that is me.

This story, like my life is still evolving, still unfolding but this story is meant to serve as a lighthouse for those still lost in dark turbulent seas. I am here to tell you that survival is not only possible but more than that, surviving a traumatic past can actually become the foundation of a thriving future.

Follow the light that this story was intended to shine, it shines especially for you.

SPECIAL THANKS

&

ACKNOWLEDGMENTS

I'd like to acknowledge some special people who helped to make this book a reality.

To the many photographers who have taken such great pictures of this incredible journey that I have been on, some of which are in the book; I say a heartfelt THANK –YOU

Mike Cameron

Ben Washington

Cyndi Ingle

Suzanne Steenkist

Dan Jelly and Wendy Schneider

There are so many people to thank that have entered my life and helped to change the trajectory. These people are forever in my heart and my gratitude is unending for all they have done.

A special thanks to Shelley Marshall for encouraging me and introducing me to Tracey Erin Smith of SOULO Theatre where the play BorderLineMe was born.

To my director, Learie McNicolls who has always had my back and to Lisa Millar who handles the public relations end of things, I'd be lost without you.

To my mom Gail and her husband Alan, thank you so much for being here for me now.

To my dear friend LaurelAnn Stead-Prociuk, thank you for everything you have done, your friendship means the world to me.

And of course my biggest thank you go to my daughter Skye who is my consistent motivating factor in life and my partner Sammy who loves and accepts me for who I am.

I could not be luckier or more blessed than to be surrounded and supported by such love.

From the bottom of my heart

THANK YOU

This book was the hardest thing I ever done

even harder than living it

because back then I was a million miles removed from myself

Disconnected disassociation surrounded by giant walls

Therapy has helped me break free from the walls that once protected and isolated me.

My past has contributed to who I am. In many ways it's shaped me but I will not let it define me.

I'm done and it's now time to let it go

What I've learned despite it all will fill the pages of my second book, as I will take up space, I will no longer be small

"Never under estimate someone's ability to shine" Maya Angelou

So shine on my friends, as we all heal at our own pace, it's not a race

The only person to compete with is ourselves

Today I will try to be a better person than I was yesterday

Love Robin Zee

Made in the USA
Middletown, DE
27 July 2019